DIARY OF A MISEDUCATED BABY MAMA: THE AFTERBIRTH

Tamykah Anthony

DIARY OF A MISEDUCATED BABY MAMA: THE AFTERBIRTH

ISBN: 978-0-578-76331-6
Busy Bee Publications, LLC

usy Bee
PUBLICATIONS

DEDICATION

This book is dedicated to my inner child. It is time for me to let you go, so I can become the woman I so desperately need to be. I have tried to hold you close, thinking I was protecting you, but I am just as toxic to you as you are to me. Before I let you go, I will bring to light all the painful memories and experiences you have held for me. I will give you a voice and speak your truth.
Then release you.

DIARY OF A MISEDUCATED BABY MAMA: THE AFTERBIRTH

CONTENTS

DIARY OF A MISEDUCATED BABY MAMA:
THE AFTERBIRTH

CONTENTS

FOREWORD

A promise, a pact for you, before you begin on this ride again. Yes, Again. This piece of work has an older sibling, an origin - telling of the life and times of this force of nature and soul of souls. Tamykah Anthony, "Scientistpreneur" and author of this new concentrated piece - Diary of a MisEducated Baby Mama: The Afterbirth. This book takes you on an 8 part journey into the mind and heart of a freedom fighter and mother nurturer. From the crown of your head to the throne of your being, you are invited to the altar. You will not leave disappointed. With the complexities of the mind, this book takes a scalpel to self in 'The Surgeon', then a turn at parenting school honors in 'Summa Cum Laude', and for the foodies, 'Blackberry Molasses' has got your fix! Take a seat, tune in and buckle up for your educational trip through Diary of A Miseducated Baby Mama: The Afterbirth.

Written by Erycka DeJesus

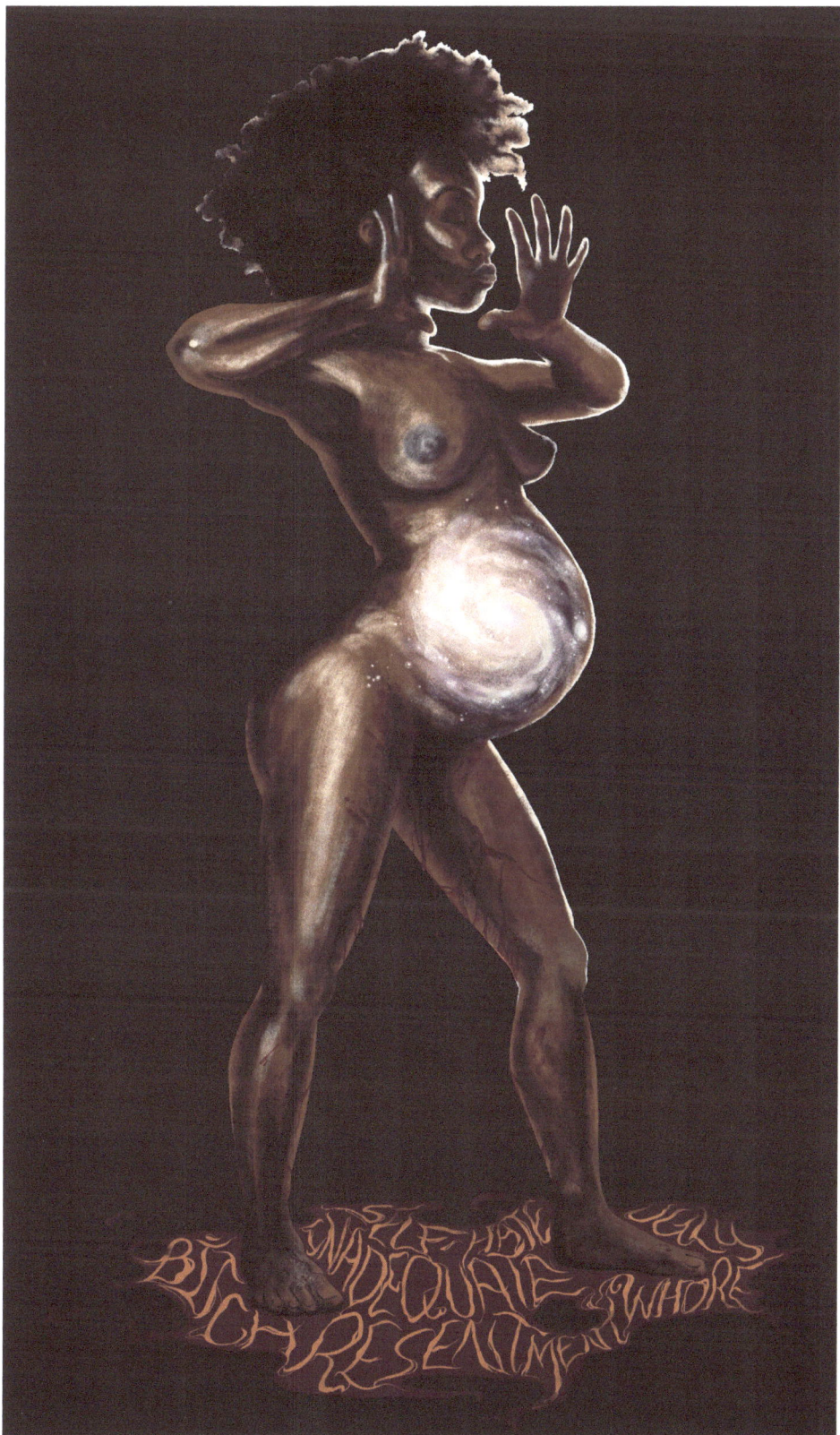

1

REFLECTIONS

Reflections to
find the points
of Inflection

RAPE

Washing my face is one of the scariest parts of my day.
Somehow soap always ends up in my eyes
Because I can't keep them closed long enough
To rinse my face.
Closing my eyes in the bathroom
Teleports me right back to that night.
Every. Single.Time.
I can still smell the anger in your labored breath.
I can still taste your bitter resentment
As you forced your tongue into my mouth.
I can still feel your hands grasping at all my open skin
Telling yourself I belonged to you.
I can still see the fear in your eyes
Knowing there was no going back.
I can still hear your words,
Reassuring me that I deserved this.
You probably thought you were my first.
That thought probably turned you on
And helped you finish.
I hope you read this and know that you were the third.
I hope you read this and take a long breath
That releases the pieces of me that you hold hostage.

RAPE

I hope you read this
And it dismantles the perverse memories of that night
That make you smile when you think of me.
I hope you read this
And know that you didn't destroy me.
In fact, I am grateful
Thank you for the hurt.
It fuels me in ways you could never comprehend.
Thank you for pushing me so close to suicide
That I learned how much I wanted to live.
And if you never read this,
I hope your future great granddaughter
Finds comfort in the words of this poem
After her first rape,
So I can save her from having a third.

MY WEDDING DAY

I felt beautiful that day. I looked at myself in the mirror and found beauty in every feature, every line, every blemish. Every heartache now made sense. Every broken heart now had purpose. All my salty tears of sadness had pooled together over the course of my 30 years to form a bright blue ocean filled with colorful fish illuminated by the sun.

As I stood in front of my bathroom mirror on my wedding day, before the makeup or the dress, I felt beautiful and full of light.The makeup artist was in the living room with my two younger sisters, my mother and her friend, my maternal grandmother, my maid of honor, my future niece in law, my then 2 year old son and then 12 year old daughter. I was in the bathroom, about to put in my contacts so I could have my makeup done.

I looked at my reflection in the mirror and smiled at her. I smiled so hard that almost all my teeth were visible, something I rarely do.

MY WEDDING DAY

I have always secretly hated the gaps between my teeth so smiling has always felt uncomfortable. I smiled and she smiled back. She had been through so much and that was my way of letting her know that everything would be okay from now on. Memories of my previous birthdays were laced with broken promises, tears and messed up plans. So when we decided to get married on my 30th birthday, I just knew this would be the beginning of beautiful birthdays and memorable anniversaries. As I looked at her through my glasses, I noticed a fuzzy smudged area on the top right of my vision. I thought nothing of it since I was taking my glasses off anyway and chocked it up to a fingerprint on the lens.

I opened the cabinet as I took off my glasses and retrieved my contact lenses. I closed the mirror and was face to face with her again. I had worn glasses most of my adult life and was still getting used to contacts and the idea of sticking things into my eyes, so I had been experimenting with different methods of inserting them.

MY WEDDING DAY

What had been working best for me was closing one eye while putting the contact into the other eye. I closed my right eye as I brought the lens close to my left eye. Looking in the mirror for guidance, I suddenly realized that I could not see my peripheral area on the right. I couldn't even see my finger holding the contact lens on the right side of my face. There was literally an entire area of my vision that was blurry and missing. I jumped from fear and as I reopened my right eye, I saw the contact slip off my finger and go down the drain of my bathroom sink.

Anyone who truly knows me knows what happens when I get scared, nervous or embarrassed. It has been the same reaction since I was a little girl and the same reaction I had in that moment. My heart started pounding so hard inside my chest that I could hear it in the silence of the bathroom. Then my "signature" top lip sweating ensued. I could feel the little beads of sweat quickly forming in that area between my top lip and nose.

MY WEDDING DAY

I immediately felt light headed and tried to grip the edge of the bathroom sink with my hands, but almost fell back. I didn't realize that my palms had also joined the sweat party and were now close to dripping with sweat, making it impossible to grip anything.

I sat on the toilet, rolled off some toilet paper to wipe my face and hands and just sat there for what felt like an eternity trying to calm myself down. I got up and went back to face the mirror.I closed my left eye and then smiled again, not as big as before , but smiled in relief. My vision was fine. This relief was short-lived when I closed the right eye, as I had done minutes before while putting in the contacts, and realized my right peripheral was gone again.

THE PAINTER

I gave you the paintbrush,
Stood in front of you naked
And told you to make me beautiful.
You painted my dark lips a pucker perfect red and smiled,
So I smiled.
You filled in the indentations in my skin
And made my stretch marks disappear.
You smiled, so I smiled
You filled in the gaps in my smile
And lightened my dark gums.
You smiled, so I smiled
This went on for years
Every Time I wanted to feel beautiful,
I brought you the palette of colors
And you whipped out your handy paintbrush
And made me your canvas.
One day, I looked in the mirror
And couldn't find myself anymore
Why couldn't you tell me I was already perfect?

SUMMA CUM LAUDE

3 children

3 different fathers

1 mother

What kind of narrative does your mind create?

She searched for "family" in her family

And couldn't find it.

So she created her own.

Armed with a fertile womb and a loving heart

MisEducated Baby Mama

18

27

31

Three decades

Three Trimesters of Life

Three Trimesters of Education

I'm a Senior now

Time to graduate

With Honors

MY SUN

Sometimes I watch you sleep
And guilt floods my spirit.
I hope you never know there was a time I didn't want you,
Even as you were growing inside me.
As my belly grew,
My anxiety grew
My anger grew
My hatred grew
I imagined you swimming
In a sea of noxious amniotic fluid
Feeding on my toxic thoughts.
In my third trimester,
I was finally able to separate
Me being your mother
From the hurt of your father.
I look at you now
Beautiful
Peaceful
Intelligent
Caring
Strong
You are my hopes and dreams for the Black Man

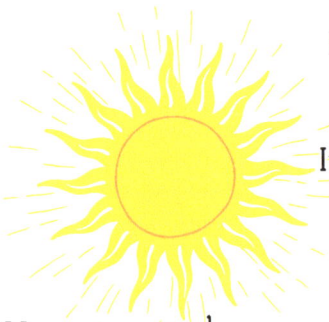

DRAWZ

Our love was like a hurricane
Raging destructive winds on the outside
Calm and peaceful whispers on the inside
In retrospect, I know you loved me with all you had
You loved the woman you knew I would become
I wish you could see her now
I wish I could have seen her then
You would be proud
R.I.P.

WHO WOULD I BE

Who would I be
If the first man to call me beautiful was my Father?

Who would I be
If my mother was the first to say "I love you"?

Who would I be
If I didn't search for my worth in the words of others?

Who would I be
If I believed in myself

As I evolve into who I will become
I Accept who I am

SECOND BEST

Life conditioned me to never go for First Place in anything
To never feel special
I remember getting straight A's
And still being told "You could do better"
And being so confused
I have spent my whole life
trying to better my best.
In search of unattainable perfection
I wear disappointment different than most
I wear it like a badge of honor
Proudly displaying it to remind myself and others
That I'm not worth it
But...
Some days I don't want to borrow from someone else
Or 'take what I get'
Or have people pick the parts of me they want to have
And then have to convince myself that's what I deserve
Because that feels better
Than me knowing I deserve more and accepting less.
Some Days, I just want something that belongs to me
That I can tap into when I need it
Some days, I want to win

2

RETALIATION

Retaliation is only
a distraction
from healing

TROPHIES

Hurting me is like an Olympic sport to you
And you have won at every level
You took Bronze when you called me your nasty bitch.
You took Silver when you desecrated my womb.
You took Gold when you said Fuck Me,
but still wanted to fuck me
Where do you hide your medals so she doesn't see them?

WASTE

When I gotta say
"Fuck this Dude!"
When I ain't even get to
Fuck. This. Dude.

LITTER BUG

Why is it always easier to throw trash on the sidewalk if
you see that others have already made it unclean.
It's like one wrapper becomes inconsequential when
staring at an already cluttered space.
When you stare at my face, do you see that now
invisible black eye I got at 18?
When you speak to my vagina, does she share with you
those times she had unwelcome visitors?
When you lick my ears, can you taste all the broken
promises that have passed through them?
When you see me naked, do you see where all the sticks
and stones have come close to breaking bones and where
all the unkind words have stabbed me?
Do you see the mosaic of lacerations and unhealed
bruises embedded in the deep lines of my skin?
Because I'm already decorated with scars,
does that make it easier to hurt me?

MISOGYNY PT. 3

Hey Kings,
It baffles me when men disrespect women
How do you disrespect a woman
When you basically started out as one?
Science Lesson for those who need it:
We are all built from the same genetic blueprint
After your Daddy's seed found a permanent home
In your Mama's Earth,
Your genitalia was phenotypically female.
Lift your testicles up and note that line.
That is where your labia fused together
I mean,
Have you ever considered why you even have nipples?
Honor your feminine energy
Your masculinity is derived from a feminine source
Eve came from Adam's rib?
NAH

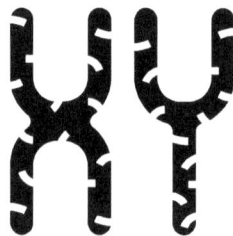

CURRENCY

There's no price tag on it
But you always want the sale price
Giving you a discount
Would require me to depreciate my own value
And I'm just not willing to do that....
Again

UNHINGED

I wonder if my tears taste different
When I cry over you
I wonder if my nectar tastes different
When I think of you
The composition of what flows out of me when triggered
by the complexities of emotion spurred by you....
Is different every time
Sometimes it's sweet
Sometimes it's bitter
Sometimes it smells like fresh cut flowers
Sometimes it smells like decomposing flesh
It's like an unstable isotope
Undergoing spontaneous nuclear decay
Spewing radioactive particles
Toxic to everyone who gets too close

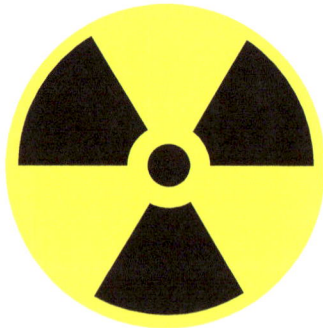

PRINCIPLES

Self Love and Reflection
I love myself
I see others as a reflection of self
I can intentionally do no harm to others
Because I love myself
And I see others as a reflection of self

TRIGGERS

The word sexy
Triggers memories of childhood
Being accused of 'acting sexy' or 'being fresh'
When I had no idea what the words even meant
Just to cover up the inappropriate lustful intentions
Of Grown Ass Men

The smell of baking bread
Triggers memories of back home
Waking up to the warm aromas of Granny's baking
Anticipating the taste
Of homemade bread with melted butter

The word Daddy
Triggers an emotional roller coaster ride with flashbacks
Of tear-filled cries for my own Daddy
And guilt-filled tears as I watched my children
Cry for their absent Daddies

3

REMISSION

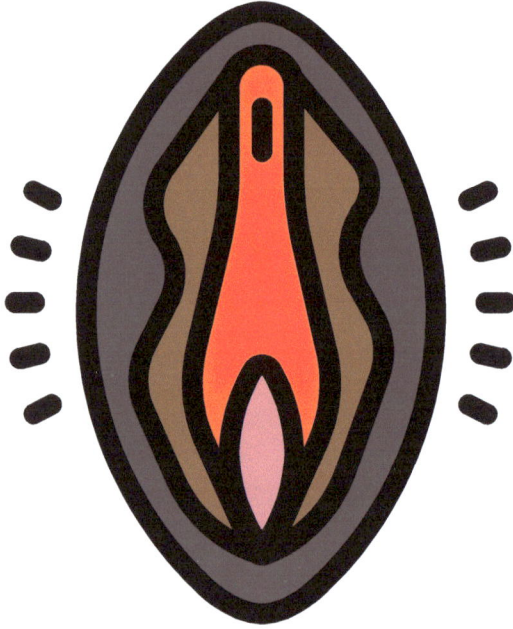

Remission is the temporary suspension of pain

CONFUSED TOUCH

Your forehead kisses and long hugs melt away bad days.
When you call me beautiful, it soothes the broken little
girl inside me who didn't hear it enough.
In your arms, I learned what safety feels like.
Why wouldn't I call you Daddy?
Your salt and pepper beard tickles the nerves
on my inner thigh
Sending shock waves throughout my body
that could compete with an earthquake.
You never stick around for the aftershocks though....
Your hands are rough, but your touch is soft.
Your fingers draw imaginary circles around my areola
Tracing lifelines and lifetimes
Our lifetimes
Because our Stars have aligned in several.
Your lips leave a trail of kisses starting on my neck
just behind my ear traveling down to my lower back.
Telling stories
Your stories
Stories of your life before I was born
Why wouldn't I call you Daddy?

CONFUSED TOUCH

I watch you get dressed
and admire the strength in your back.
The lips that delivered passionate kisses moments before
Now taste different.
Your sweet kisses now salty .
They taste like disappointment.
Your lips say I love you,
but your fingers now trace words
I've heard many times before:
"You're not good enough"
In those moments, I am no longer a woman.
I am that little girl.
I wonder if you notice the transformation.
The little girl who never felt good enough.
The little girl who wasn't hugged enough.
The little girl who no one ever called beautiful.
The little girl who was taught
to feel ashamed of her dark skin.
The little girl who's Daddy wasn't there.

CONFUSED TOUCH

The most naked I've ever felt in my life
is when you walk away.
You take pieces of me every time.
I never watch you leave.
I turn my back so I don't see your back to me.
So I have no memory of it.
So I can't replay it over and over
Enough times to build up the strength to let you go.
Every time I think I've hit my limit,
You push it a little further
So far that I don't know how to come back
Truth is....
Every time you leave,
There's a piece of me that secretly wishes
you will come back and say,
"I'm staying"
So I can finally stop calling you Daddy

30

AFTERTASTE

As you try to wash away any evidence of me
down the hotel bathroom sink,
I roll over to your side of the bed,
now cold and empty.
The wet spots where our DNA mingled not yet dry.
The pillow still full of your scent
So I take a deep breath and take you in
So you can fill me up once again.
Pun intended.
The faucet still running
as you use the soap-laden washcloth
to retrace trails my tongue drew on your body.
I sometimes wonder
if she can detect the subtle aftertaste
of my nectar in your breath.
If she can faintly smell the virgin coconut oil
infused with lavender and geranium
that I drench my skin in...
Just the way you like it

THIRST TRAP

I thought cravings only happened with food
But...
My ears crave the vibration of your voice.
When you speak life into me,
Your words are inspiration for precipitation,
Causing teary waterfalls and yoni drips like a leaky faucet

My eyes crave the vision
Of skinny dipping in the warm salty oceans
That are your beautiful brown eyes.
My soul craves our nocturnal duets,
Conversations consecrated by the moon and stars,
With crickets, katydids and your boyish laughter
Providing background music.
The arch in my back craves your fingertips
Playing staccato notes that rise to a crescendo,
building anticipation....

POSSESSION

I realize now I am a mystery
To insecure and unsecured men.
And what they do not understand,
Becomes Intriguing to them
They attempt to possess me,
To study me
Inside and Out
They perform exploratory surgery
With their weak phalluses
Trying to find the breaking points inside me.
They attempt to permanently tattoo my womb
With their seminal fluids
To use me as a vessel for their seeds
Because that is the ultimate form of
Patriarchal Possession right?
And when they can't possess me,
They attempt to destroy me
So that no one else will want me

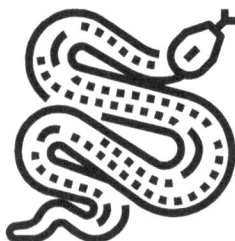

DISTRACTIONS

As I get closer to manifesting my wildest dreams
Fear sets in
I start looking for distractions
And the Universe provides...

LOW VIBRATIONS

I don't remember what the original sin was
But I've been punishing myself for it.
Seeking hurt and disappointment anywhere I can find it
Feeling relief when I experience pain
Using the wounding words of others
To beat myself up

Sometimes I feel unworthy of getting my sight back
Like the Creator should have chosen someone else
To receive that blessing
The pressure I feel some days is immeasurable

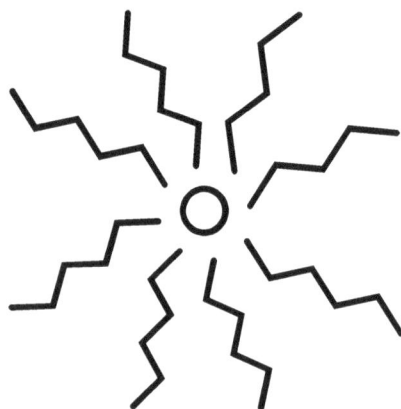

SELF LOVE

Do I love myself?

I mean...

I like the smoothness of my skin

I like the strength in my calves

I like the deep lines in the palms of my hands

I like the definition in my cheekbones

I like that others find safety and compassion in my eyes

I like that my touch has the ability to calm

But,

Do I love myself?

WARPED

I saw you Imperfect
Like a crooked tree
And I thought
If I could only straighten your crookedness,
You would be perfect
So I did
Turns out,
I was the crooked one that needed straightening
And I ruined a perfectly good tree

4

RESILIENCE

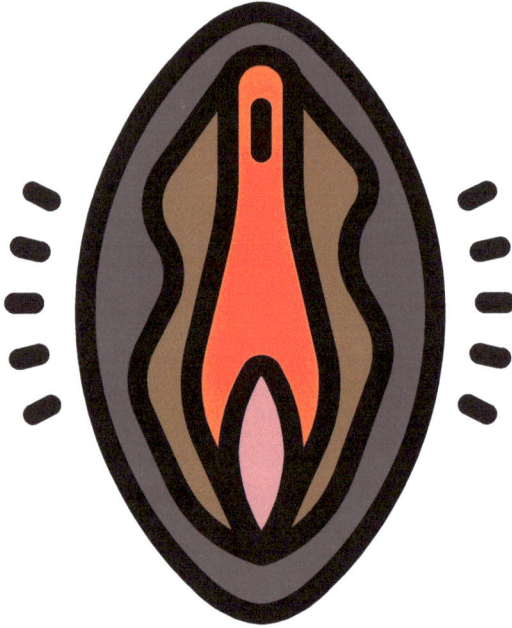

Resilience is the backbone of the Black Woman

FORAGER BEE

Your straw-like tongue spreads my thighs.
Like the delicate petals of a flower.
My juices provide the nectar for your honey.
I give it to you freely.
Knowing the more nectar I give,
The sweeter your honey will be.
Fatherhood is the honey.
Some days,
It feels like the sweet nectar of my vagina
Is the lifeline of your fatherhood.
You move on to the next flower.....
Now, Queen Bee must turn into a worker bee
to take care of the hive.

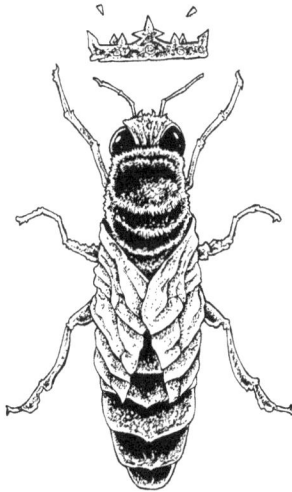

PURPLE HEELS

I used to pass this shoe store everyday on my way to work. Even when I was running late, I always took a few moments to look in the display window. See, there were these purple shoes. They were the most beautiful shoes I had ever laid eyes on and I would stop and stare at them in admiration. I wanted those shoes soooo badly.
Without looking at the price tag, I convinced myself that I could not afford them. For months, the same routine. Just looking and wanting .
One day, I got off the train earlier than usual and I was extra excited because I would have even more time to stare in the store window. There was a man there, in my usual spot. Annoyed, I stood next to him to look in the store window. He turned, looked at me and smiled. Out of nowhere, he handed me a folded piece of paper and then walked away before I could give it back. I opened the note, and read:
"I've been watching you for months. The Purple Shoes are paid for. They're all yours. Enjoy"
In utter disbelief, I stared in the direction he walked in, but he was already gone. "This must be some kind of joke", I thought. But what if it wasn't?

PURPLE HEELS

Forgetting all about clocking in on time at work, I rushed into the store, but stopped short inside the doorway. The air felt different in here. In that moment, I realized that in all the months I had admired these shoes, I had never been inside the store. I had never touched the shoes or tried them on. Why is that?

I walked up to the counter, unsure of what to say to the salesperson. Before I could utter a word, she smiled and asked, "What size?" I don't even remember giving her my size but a few moments later, she returned with a box. Would you believe I didn't try them on?

After wanting these shoes for all this time, I didn't even open the box. I took the shoes home and put them on my shelf and they stayed there for weeks. An intense anxiety would come over me every time I looked at the box.

Sabotaging thoughts consumed me:
What if they didn't fit?
What if I couldn't walk in them?
What if I couldn't find an outfit to match?
What if no one liked them on me?

PURPLE HEELS

Isn't it amazing how we get comfortable "wanting"?
I spent more time wanting them than I did preparing to
have them, because I never truly thought they would be
mine.

SANKOFA

Dear Ancestors,

Why do we pray for them
While they prey on us?

We call on you for
Guidance
Strength
And an intolerable spirit

Signed,
Your Lost Children

BLACK MOTHERHOOD

The first time your heart beat
Was while I carried you in my womb.
My greatest fear
Is feeling your last heartbeat
While I carry you in my arms.
When you were born,
I held your bloodied bodies
As air filled your lungs
And you cried for the comfort of Mommy's bosom.
My greatest fear
Is holding your bloodied bodies
Against my bosom
As you take your last breath.

TOUGH LOVE

The hardest part about love
Isn't learning how to love
Or learning how to be loved
The hardest part is learning that
In the truest form of love,
You can't have one without the other

BROWN SKINNED GIRL

The Black Woman is the source of Infinite Love and Beauty
The potential energy you harness
Is in the crevices of your Blackness.
They will tell you that you can't do it
Because THEY can't do it
But, I see you Sis
I see YOU
Your strength is in your voice
Strong enough to lift and uplift
The heaviest man with just your words
Your power is in your tongue
And sometimes knowing that your true sovereignty
Is cradled in your silence
Under the laid edges and perfect brows,
I see YOU
And one day,
I pray that you see YOU too

EYES WIDE SHUT

Losing the ability to see the outside world
Left me only one choice:
To look within
I was in a dark room with myself

The gift of sight was a distraction
There was always something to look at
Colors
People
Sunsets
Distractions from self

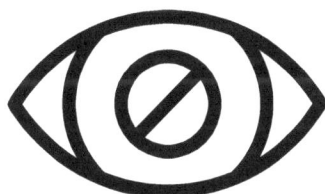

WINDOWS

My jagged edges are like tiny windows
Giving you an unobstructed view inside me
If you take the time to look closely enough

If I didn't have broken pieces,
How would your light get in?

5

RELEASE

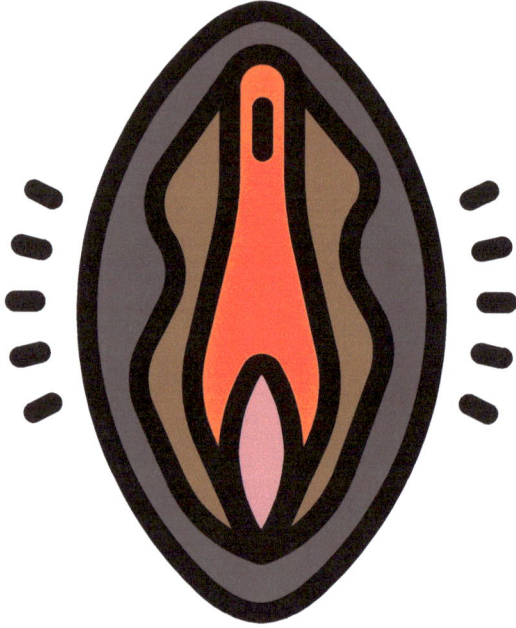

Release of all
things that no
longer serve me

PRISONER

My dark skin is fitting.
Because that's where you keep me.
In the darkest parts of your existence.
My ebony skin camouflaged in the deepest recesses of your
thoughts and desires.
For a while I was comfortably uncomfortable there.
Like a prisoner in solitary,
Waiting for my one hour out with you.
For a while,
that one hour was enough to keep me going.
But now my claustrophobia is acting up.

MOMMY ISSUES

We go so hard for 'Daddy Issues'
But the root of Daddy's issues
Usually comes from his Mama anyway.
A Mama who raised him alone
Seasoning his food with the resentment and bitterness
Of single motherhood.
A Mama who worked too hard
And never quite got the Provider/Nurturer balance right,
Because it was never meant for one person.
A Mama who couldn't let him suckle at her breast
Because the bills had already drained the life out of her.
He goes into the world
MisEducated by porn
Misogyny infused in his DNA
Misguided Masculinity
Unaware that he is a King
Unable to recognize a Queen

TO MY UNHEALED SELF

I like this one, Sis
He has real potential
Please let me have him

Please don't pop up when we make love to remind me
of times my body was abused
Please don't whisper sour memories in one ear while he's
whispering sweet nothings in the other

I like this feeling Sis
I know I have real potential
Please let me have this...

THE SURGEON

For years, I had put band aids on open wounds
that needed major surgery
I had to become my own surgeon to heal
Opening myself up,
Searching for all the hemorrhages needing hemostasis
The tumors that needed excising
The gashes that needed suturing
And the superficial cuts that just needed Love
Through this process,
I discovered what pain really is
Now, the scars don't remind me of the trauma
like the wounds used to
The scars remind me of my strength
Healing isn't pretty,
But it IS beautiful
Is healing a lifelong process?
Do we ever get to say:
"I AM HEALED"
I don't know
But my scalpel is always ready

"TILL DEATH DO US PART"

As I spread the ashes of my marriage
In the waters near where I took my vows,
I wondered if they would sink or float.
They sunk.
It was then I realized the true meaning of those vows:
"Till Death do us Part"
I could not innerstand
How two people could be stuck together
I think most interpret those words as:
Until the man or the woman dies.
I disagree
When two people marry,
They create a separate entity: their marriage
Like a plant,
It needs to be watered, fed, given light and loved on
And like a plant,
Without this level of care,
It withers and dies.
At that point,
No amount of water or light can revive it
Till Death Do Us Part

UNTITLED

You didn't see me
You were in love with the idea of me
You salivated at how possessing me
Would increase your net worth
You wanted me to shine bright
So you could use my light to illuminate you
You don't get a chapter in my book
You haven't earned a spot
In my Table of Contents
This poem wont even have a title
You know who you are

COMPOST PROJECT

I imagine these words will transcend the current reality
A reality that has most of the world
Distanced and Inside.
A reality where staying away from friends and family
Is the best way to keep them safe.
A reality where single mothers are juggling
Working from home,
Homeschooling their children
Keeping food and shelter intact
While keeping fear of the unknown locked up in places
their children wont find it.
Some would call it a war.
If you are that father that hasn't
In the least
Checked on the well-being of your children.
If you planted a seed in the Earth
But aren't making sure it gets
Water, Sunlight and Love,
Do the world a favor:
Compost Yourself!

COMPOST PROJECT

Let the community turn you into human compost
so that the Earth can use up all the organic parts of you.
At least, this way,
You will be purposeful

RELEASE

My body dissolved your hate
Like an unfertilized egg
I held your vile words
In the lining of my uterus
and shed them
With my last period
I release you

6

REBIRTH

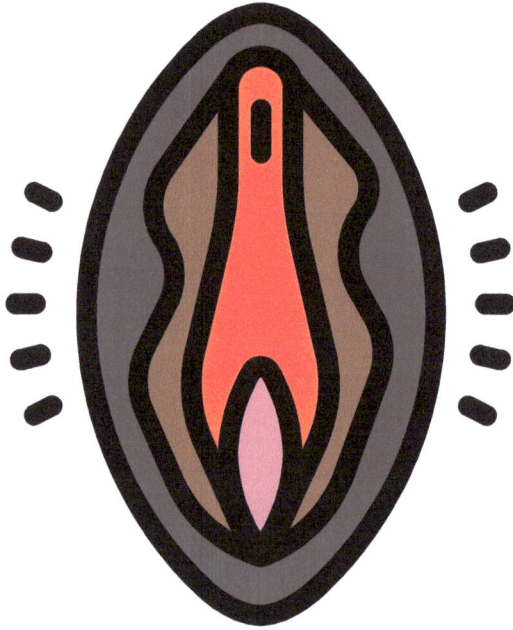

Rebirth is Reincarnation of self

To My Unborns

My fertile Earth
But not all seedlings got to flower
For some, the Earth couldn't sustain them
For others, the Earth wouldn't sustain them
Because I felt she shouldn't sustain them
But each one has left an irreplaceable imprint in the soil
where nothing else can grow
Hard imprints
Hardened by guilt,
Hardened by relief
Hardened by regret
And although no flowers will ever bloom,
my tears still feed the Earth there,
allowing those feelings to grow
They consume me
The memories I will never have of you consume me
Due dates turned to birthdays
that will never be celebrated
Some days when it's quiet,
I hear whispers of "Mommy"
and wonder if that's you calling me
or my guilt and regret playing tricks

TO MY UNBORNS

Please forgive me
and give me permission to forgive myself
R.I.P.
Release.
Inner.
Pain.
Rest In Peace
Asè

RIDE OR DIE

You hitchhiked a ride
On my road to Self Love
And we ended up having the same destination:
Loving ME

METAMORPHOSIS

Does a caterpillar know that she's about to be a butterfly?

While the caterpillar crawls slowly on her belly,
Does she look up at the beautifully winged butterflies
And know that she too will become one?

And, when she emerges from her cocoon as a butterfly,
Does she look down at the slow crawling caterpillars
And remember that part of her life?

Do caterpillars and butterflies communicate?
Can a caterpillar teach humility to a butterfly?
Can a butterfly give a caterpillar HOPE?

PERSPECTIVE

There have been times
when I thought I was buried
But ...
After
A Little water
A Little sunlight
A Little Love
I realized I wasn't buried
I was planted.
Growth

DIVORCE

This may be the shortest piece in the book
I divorced you
When I married my bliss
Love and Light
Always

LOVE'S ILLUSION

What does it mean to fall in love?

Sounds dangerous

Like an accident

Like I slipped on a banana peel

And fell into a puddle of 'LOVE'

Wouldn't you rather

RISE in love?

Be ELEVATED by love?

ASCEND with love?

GEOMETRY

You're a square trying to fit inside my circle
Those four corners digging into me
As you try to force your way into my space
Knowing you can't fit
Knowing you are hurting me

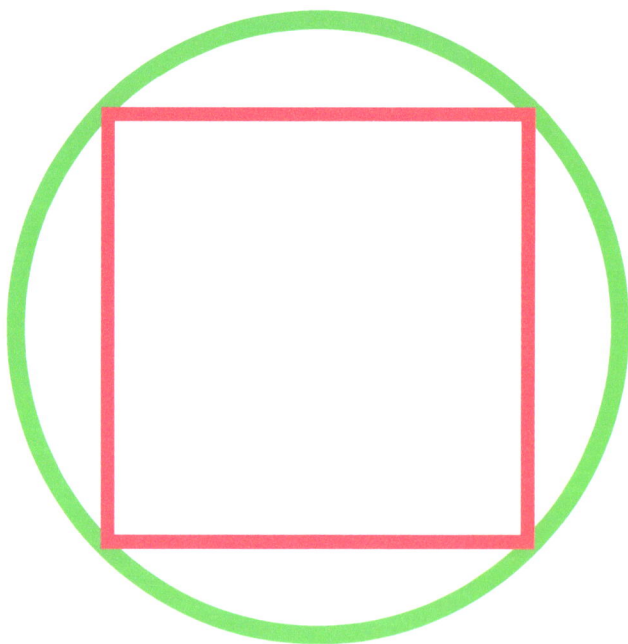

BLACK MAN

Black Man,
Do you truly see ME?
I am not the Angry Black Woman
I am the Tired Black Woman
Always seeking safe spaces to bask in my Femininity
I am not the Bitter Black Woman
I am the Confused Black Woman
Trying to figure out why you left me alone to raise a child.
I am not the Jaded Black Woman
I am the Guarded Black Woman
How do I shield myself
From the sharp fragments of your brokenness
AND be compassionate to your struggle
Black Man,
Do you see ME?

7

RADIANCE

Radiance is realizing you are the light you seek

TO MY FUTURE KING

I'm not ready
Not ready for the unconditional love that I know would
beam out of you like the sun's rays ready to envelop me in
the warmth of your embrace.
I would find a way to sabotage it

I'm not ready
Not ready for the way I know you would stare deeply into
my eyes, climb into my soul and take refuge there while
protecting me from the inside out.
I would look away because I wouldn't feel deserving

I'm not ready
Not ready for the way I know you would trace my stretch
marks and appreciate the sacrifices my body has made to
ensure the immortality of our people.
I would push your hand away and cover myself feeling
shame

TO MY FUTURE KING

I'm not ready
Not ready for you to not judge my past but innerstand
even the dark pieces of my journey that lead me to you.
I would tell you I have too much baggage for you.

I'm not ready
Not ready for you to be mesmerized by the layers and
degrees of melanin in my skin and tell me how you've seen
me in your dreams and wondered if such a beautiful
creature even existed.
I would laugh nervously and accuse you of lying.

I'm not ready
Not ready for you to tell me how beautiful the gaps in my
teeth are because they give you a window to my soul
I would look down and cover my mouth self-consciously

TO MY FUTURE KING

I'm not ready
Not ready for the way you would find peace nestled in my breast listening to the binaural beats created by the simultaneous vibrations of my now healed heart beat and the calm inflections of my voice as I play with your ear lobe and caress your face
I would tell you I need some space

But one day I will be ready
To be so open that all my scars show,
but also vulnerable enough to let you kiss them.
To be loving on myself so much so that it teaches you how to love on me
To be so compassionate that I forgive myself for not being ready sooner
Until we meet, I will continue to be patient with myself
Until we meet, keep dreaming about me, King

GODDESS

Your hair is your crown
Your ass is your throne
The universe is your kingdom
Do you even know how powerful you are?
Mother,
The nectar between your legs
Immortalizes seeds into generations
Healer,
The honey in your bosom
Carries the antidote for humanity
Storyteller,
The lines in your face tell the stories of our ancestors
The lines on your womb tell the stories of the future
Your hair is your crown
Your ass is your throne
The universe is your kingdom
Do you even know how powerful you are?

75

LOVE LANGUAGE

What language do you feel LOVE in?
Words of Affirmation
Acts of Service
Receiving Gifts
Quality Time
Physical Touch
I don't know what my language is
I have felt so unlovable at times
That I just took whatever they're willing to give,
As long as they put a bow on it
And called it LOVE
As I innerstand LOVE now,
Love is a frequency
Like a radio station
As long as you're tuned in
And ready to receive,
You will
Feel Love
Embody Love
Resonate Love
Emit Love
Love speaks ONE language
Love IS the language

TAUREAN WOMAN

Sharp horns with a soft underbelly
Stubborn yet submissive
Diligent yet indolent
Sarcastic yet sensitive
Cool yet compassionate
Free spirited yet guarded
Her uncontrollable raging anger
Is matched only by how deeply she loves
Have you ever been loved by Taurean woman?
Ruled by Venus,
Guided by Amun Ra
She is the Goddess of Love
Patient
Kind
Supportive
Nurturing
Loyal
Intriguing
Delicate

TAUREAN WOMAN

Have you ever lost a Taurean woman?
You will spend the rest of your life
Looking for pieces of her in every other woman,
Disappointed every time
No matter how much you chase her,
Once she's gone, she's gone forever

MY CRUSH

When I look at you,
I imagine your sweat tastes like
the salty waters of Yemaya's playground

When you are near me,
I take deeper breaths in
Hoping I can inhale some of your exhale

When I hear your voice,
I don't get butterflies
I feel full blown tsunamis in my womb

UNCONDITIONAL

I love you
In spite of yourself
Despite yourself

I love you
Even as you do everything in your power
To make me hate you
You don't truly believe you deserve my love.
You would rather hurt me
Than have me Love you

But....I love you
In spite of yourself
Despite yourself
I love you

VAGINA DIALOGUES

I'm sorry for not checking in with you
Before we had visitors
I'm sorry for dressing you in lace underwear
Thinking I needed to make you more appealing,
When I was only irritating you.
I'm sorry for the waxing fails
You didn't deserve that
Thank you for my Motherhood
For granting my offspring safe passage into the world
Thank you for righting my wrongs
For being so forgiving,
For always snapping back
Even after I used you as currency
To buy comfort from others
Thank you for all you have done for me
Now, it's my time to take better care of you
Sis, we about to have some real fun together

JEALOUSY

I get jealous of other people's experience of me
I want to feel my own love
I want to feel my own touch
I want to feel my own kisses
I want to see myself
Through the eyes of those who adore me

8

RAPTURE

Rapture is
Bliss,
manifested

INTIMACY

When I can taste your words.
When I can smell your thoughts.
When I can feel your scent.
When you touch me,
It creates a vibration I can actually hear.
Yes I can hear your touch.
When I take in your scent,
It manifests the clearest memories
Of past lifetimes together.
So wrapped up in each other,
I don't know where you end and I begin.
We transcend time and space.
We transcend the five senses.
You and I create a sixth sense
That allows us to touch
In ways fingers can't comprehend.
Where we can sit in silence for hours,
And communicate without uttering a word.
Where you can incite me to climax with just your eyes.

INTIMACY

We are not married,
But our spirits have taken vows we are not aware of.
We are not soulmates,
But our souls mate effortlessly.
We have never fallen in love
We rise in love
Lifted by the high tides produced when our moons coalesce.
A luminescence powerful enough to compete with the sun.
Your high is like no other.

BLACKBERRY MOLASSES

I have vivid memories of my future with you
Of things that have yet to happen

On an island devouring over-ripe fresh picked mangoes
Juices dripping between my fingers and down my arm
Droplets collecting on the tip of my elbow
Before forming sticky pools of mango nectar on my thighs

Us spending weeks in tropical paradise
Watching your skin transform
from the color of orange blossom honey
to the color of Blackberry Molasses...
the kind that doesn't cause
Heartache and Pain

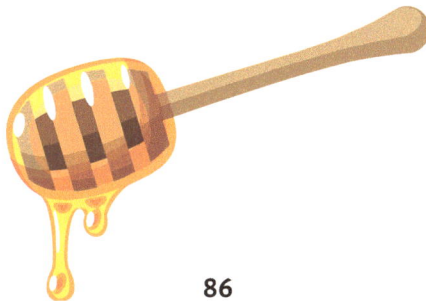

BLISS

Sitting between your legs
My cheek resting on your inner thigh
While you grease my scalp
And brush my hair

Rubbing my growing belly
Dozing into blissful dreams
As you massage my temples
With intermittent forehead kisses

REGURGITATED RECIPROCITY

I wanna love on myself
Then have this newly loved self pour love into you
And then have you,
After being loved by my newly loved self,
Love Me
Damn, what would that feel like?

WELCOME TO HEAVEN

You said you have never met God
But I beg to differ
You say you've never heard God
But my voice strokes your eardrum daily
You say you've never smelled God
But the way your eyes roll when you inhale my essence...
You say you've never felt God
But when we touch,
Your first utterance is "Oh, God"
You say you've never seen God
But your eyes have witnessed me perform miracles
You say you've never tasted God
But...
You already know

NOTES TO SELF

NOTE: You matter because you are matter in all forms
Strong Earth
Untamed Water
Kinetic Air
And sometimes you're Fire
In a transient state
No fixed volume
No fixed shape
You matter because you are antimatter
The most expensive substance on Earth
Otherworldly
Ethereal
NOTE: When a man asks,
"What qualities are you looking for in a man?"
You will respond,
"The same ones he's looking for in me.
We will know when we find each other"
NOTE: You are DOPENESS, Personified
Value yourself

ODE TO BABA SEBI

Everyday, when I open my eyes,
There's a moment
When everything is blurry
As my eyes adjust to the rays of light
Then I think of you, Baba Sebi
And gratitude fills my spirit

For 8 months,
Light turned to Darkness
As I lost the ability to see.
Thank you for renewing my light
For giving me new vision
And for allowing my eyes to taste the sun again

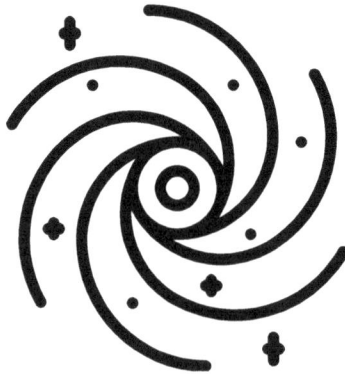

LOVE & LIGHT

Some will use my words as ammunition to load their ego
And then shoot shots of judgment at me
Not realizing they're really boomerangs
That will bounce off my renewed spirit
And return to hit them when they least expect it,
Those same ones will think they now know
The weakest parts of me
Maybe even highlighting the darkest pages
To re-read when their misery needs company.
Some will use my words to reflect on their own truths
Some who have hurt me will search for themselves
Feverishly scouring every page
Thinking each word is about them.
Nevertheless,
Love and Everlasting Light

About the Author

Tamykah Anthony is a passionate award winning Forensic Toxicologist. She used her unique science background to create a natural product line, Xanthines All Natural Products (@xanthinesallnaturalproducts), that provides natural and affordable non-toxic alternatives to personal care products. She is also the Founder of Xanthines Cafe AKA Camp Wakanda (@camp_wakanda), a camp created to teach Black and Brown children about their innate superpowers through Science, Technology, Engineering/Entrepreneurship, the Arts, Math and more. She serves as a mentor, role model and inspiration to children and women, specifically those in the Brooklyn communities where she grew up. She is a mom to 3 amazing children: Nevaeh, Sameer and Usha. In her spare time, she enjoys writing, listening to music, doing crossword puzzles and creating fun activities for her homeschooled children.

www.ingramcontent.com/pod-product-compliance
Lightning Source LLC
Chambersburg PA
CBHW041424090426
42742CB00030BA/9